Listening Up!

J. CHARLES CALLANAN

Listening Up!

Everyday Wisdom for a Noisy World

NOVALIS

© 2008 Novalis, Saint Paul University, Ottawa, Canada

Cover design and Layout: Pascale Turmel, Audrey Wells
Layout: Julie-Anne Lemire, Francine Petitclerc

Business Offices:

Novalis Publishing Inc.

10 Lower Spadina Avenue, Suite 400
Toronto, Ontario, Canada
M5V 2Z2

Novalis Publishing Inc.

4475 Frontenac Street
Montréal, Québec, Canada
H2H 2S2

Phone: 1-800-387-7164
Fax: 1-800-204-4140
E-mail: books@novalis.ca
www.novalis.ca

Library and Archives Canada Cataloguing in Publication

Callanan, J. Charles (John Charles), 1936–
     Listening up! : everyday wisdom for a noisy world / J. Charles Callanan.

ISBN 978-2-89646-003-8

     1. Catholic Church–Prayers and devotions. 2. Meditations. 3. Christian
life–Catholic authors. I. Title.

BX2182.3.C34
2008   242   C2008-901544-4

Printed in Canada.

We acknowledge the financial support of the Government of Canada through
the Book Publishing Industry Development Program (BPIDP) for our
publishing activities.

5   4   3   2   1   12   11   10   09   08

*For my wife, Patricia,
and my sons, Mark and Luke*

Contents

Introduction

Everywhere I look these days, I find people searching for spirituality. It is not a search for religion as such, but rather a search for the spiritual in life and beyond. We have ready access to information at our disposal, but find ourselves saying, in the words of a popular song, "Is that all there is?"

I believe that there is more – much more. The pieces in this book represent my attempts over the years to search for what it means to be truly human in a changing world. Our very humanness is being compromised by an increasingly impersonal culture. Does God exist? If so, does God care about me and my family? These issues are important to everybody.

I started to write these reflections in the sixties, in the now defunct *Ottawa Journal*. Later, when I returned to Newfoundland, I was invited to write for the *Diocesan Review* of Corner Brook and *The Monitor* of St. John's.

Some of these pieces were written when I was in Ottawa, working as an Oblate priest. Others I wrote after I left the ministry, returned to Newfoundland, married, had a family and worked at Memorial University in media and adult education.

It is my hope that these pieces will strike a responsive chord in readers. We are all on the same journey through this life. We are meant to help each other as we go. I hope that these meditations will be of some help in your search for meaning.

Charlie Callanan
St. John's, Newfoundland
February 2008

Everybody Talks, Nobody Listens

We teach our children how to speak, but we don't teach them how to listen. We can't possibly teach them how to listen when we ourselves do not know how to listen. The world is filled with people who talk. How far do you have to search in this life to find someone who knows how to listen?

When people gather together, everybody talks and nobody listens. Anyone who keeps eyes and ears open learns something about life and people. Most of us learn nothing, because we are not open to others.

We will never listen to others unless we are convinced of their worth. Our problem is that we have pre-judged others and have come to expect nothing from them, and so we seal up our ears and close our eyes to any truth they may have for us. This turning people off does not stop with strangers. After a while we turn our family off as well, and we do not leave our relationships open-ended. This is why we become bored with each other. We have become closed to each other and there is no more wonder within us.

Because we do not listen to each other, we miss about 80 per cent of life. We are satisfied to hear ourselves talk and that is enough for us. The more we talk without listening to others, the more empty we become. Most people abuse the gift of speech because they lack the art of listening.

Those who love us speak to us not only with words but with their whole being. Are we too concerned with our own thoughts to hear them?

God also speaks to us, not in words, but with his whole being. God speaks to us through the modern world, yet those who listen are in the minority. God speaks to us through heart transplants, through the exploration of space, through student unrest and civil rights demonstrations. God speaks to us through our pain, through our loneliness and through our alienation from other people.

Our whole society is like a gigantic cocktail party in which everybody is chattering and nobody is listening. Besides producing artificial teeth, artificial fur and artificial food, we have betrayed our humanity by producing artificial communication. By so doing, we have made loneliness a social rather than an individual reality. Through computers we have extended our central nervous system outside ourselves; we now have machines that "think." In 1968, students at Sir George Williams University destroyed such machines because, according to their thinking, people were not listening to what the students themselves were saying. Vandalism will never cure our ills, yet violence is a symptom of a world that has forgotten how to listen.

Homes change when husbands listen to wives, when wives listen to husbands and when parents listen to children.

Our world could be saved if nations listened to nations. Listening could well be our greatest untapped resource and the very key to our survival.

Being Accepted

It is a terrible thing to feel rejected. When we feel this way, we believe that people do not see any worth or value in us. It is very important for our survival as human beings to feel that we are accepted by our families, our co-workers, our friends or the members of our church. Many people go to great lengths in their attempts to be accepted by others, even if this means pretending to be someone other than their real selves.

The need to be accepted is a basic human need. Students who do not feel accepted by their teachers will not learn. People who do not feel accepted by their co-workers will deal with constant inner tension on the job.

On the other hand, being accepted gives us a feeling of self-worth. The person who deeply accepts me gives me the freedom to be myself. When I meet someone who accepts me, I have the courage to reveal myself with all my faults. I don't need to create a false image of myself to meet that person's expectations.

We all dream of meeting another person whom we can really talk to, someone who will listen to us, understand and accept us. Yet we all – especially those who feel particularly rejected and alone – forget that God accepts us completely.

Before he died, Jesus prayed to his Father that "the world might know that you love them as you love me." In other words, God loves each of us just as much as he loves his own Son, Jesus Christ. This has to be so, since God cannot do anything incompletely. He can't love us 40 or 50 per cent. If he loves, he loves 100 per cent.

It is tragic that many of us have lived all too long with an image of God as a stern judge who (we think) does not accept us or love us as we are. Our faith must carry us beyond these negative images of God to a discovery of the loving and merciful God who is revealed to us by Jesus.

Accepting Acceptance

In his book *To Love and Be Loved*, Sam Keen says that no matter what we do in life, we all seek to love and to be loved. A woman once said to him, "Outside of my parents, I have never been loved by anybody." This woman longed to make a breakthrough and to experience what it means to be loved.

Our search for love, whether we realize it or not, is always tied in with the very source of all love – God. God *is* love. In St. Augustine's words, "Our hearts are restless until they rest in you, O God."

Love is about feeling accepted for who we are. We want to be accepted by our friends and families, by a church group, by a sports team or recreational group, by the people at work, and by God. Yet even when we are accepted by others we may feel hesitant and doubtful. We find it difficult to *accept* acceptance. This is true of our relationship with God, as well. God accepts us and forgives us, but we can be more preoccupied with our own guilt or shame than we are with God.

Paul Tillich, a 20th-century Protestant theologian, defines faith as "the courage to accept acceptance."

Our problem is not our love for God; our problem concerns God's love for us. We don't really believe in it. We don't really believe that God loves us and accepts us with our doubts and our failures. That is why Tillich says that it takes courage to accept acceptance.

When we deeply believe that God loves us no matter what we have done, we gain confidence in ourselves and we are able to be more open to others. This openness in turn makes us more lovable to our friends and to all the people we meet.

Many films and books tell the stories of people who are transformed because they are loved. These stories make us feel good. In our hearts, we wish that all of life could be like this: a place where we listen to each other's stories without passing judgment and where we dry each other's tears.

Sometimes people have been hurt so much in life that they cannot reach out to others in love. Part of our job as Christians is to listen with sensitivity and understanding to those who are hurt, and help them accept that they, like we, have truly been accepted by God.

Create Community

A psychiatrist in China, writing about changes in that country, writes, "We live in an ocean of people but we are alone. People communicate so little with their neighbours now. Everyone is in charge of himself, everyone has to be independent, and it creates more inner pressure and anxiety …. Our society is radically changing and it's producing more and more stresses. It's a challenge to our traditional culture and values."

You don't have to live in China to agree with this writer. North American society is also undergoing massive changes.

Many people feel alienated and alone. They are on a survival treadmill and have long ago forgotten how to enjoy themselves and their friends.

For some, life seems to be a race to possess more and more "stuff." Our houses have become fortresses and entertainment centres. Telephone technology helps us to screen calls; we are "cocooned" in our homes, sheltered from a world that we see as less friendly than in the past.

This is a dark vision in which something is missing. We need to remind ourselves that we are Christians and that we have come from a Christian culture and world view.

The essence of a Christian culture is the focus on the community, not on the individual. If people feel alienated today, that is because they lack community or identification with community. The Church's main job is to create community and to show individuals that they are not alone in the world. Where we see people loved, cared for, housed, clothed and fed we can say, "Here is the Kingdom of God."

If our parishes are merely spiritual service stations where we go to "get communion" and come home, then our view of what it means to be a Christian is inadequate.

With fewer or even no priests or ministers in some parishes, we must take more responsibility for creating Christian community. The Church cannot go on forever if we remain passive. We must become more motivated and more involved.

Jesus, true to his promise, will be with the Church till the end of time. In the meantime, he needs our help.

Everybody is Somebody

It seems that we are lost in a sea of materialism. Many kids get too much and come to expect more. Teenagers will only wear name-brand clothes. People feel that they must always have the latest electronic gadget. Families that do not get a vacation every year feel deprived.

A materialistic society such as ours tends to make people class-conscious. The place where we work, the clothes we wear, the type of car we drive and the kind of house we live in – all these things tend to place us at a certain level in society. Some people are automatically "in" and others are "out."

Many people spend their lives trying to get "in." They are unhappy because they feel that they have missed the boat. Those who make it usually find out that there's not much going on "inside" after all.

Yet, who makes the rules? Who shapes our expectations and tells us that we are "out" if we don't have certain things? The people who hold so much power over us are a handful of brilliant, creative advertising people. Along with the writers of popular television shows, they set the trends and tell us what the "in" crowd eats, drinks and wears. Most of us are foolish enough to go along with it. We certainly don't want people to think that we never made it.

We don't measure ourselves from within. We measure ourselves by the things we have acquired.

Christianity says that everyone is accepted for who they are, regardless of wealth or talents. Jesus spent a lifetime bringing down certain misconceptions about how people should be treated. He ate with the "out" crowd and hung around with people who were pretty low on the social ladder. The "in" crowd held him in contempt. "Can anything good come out of Nazareth?" they sneered.

Many people feel that they are nobody. Yet as Christians, we believe that everybody is somebody. Everyone has worth. In giving everyone the respect that is their due as human beings, we help to build the Kingdom of God.

Time

An advertisement that caught my eye lately had to do with retirement planning. It showed a photograph of a baby with this caption: "This baby is 23,725 days from retirement." I had never thought of measuring my life in days, but the ad reminded me that my days actually are numbered.

I played with this concept and found that my mother's life consisted of 31,755 days. My father lived for 25,550 days. Jesus had a relatively short life, with approximately 12,045 days among us.

You get a strange feeling knowing that your days can be numbered. When we are young, we feel that our time is limitless – we have our whole lives ahead of us. Nobody speaks to us about limits.

Yet today we have (or think we have) so many things to do with our time that not much is left for ourselves, our family, our friends, or God.

Remember the Martha and Mary story in the gospels? Most of us today are like Martha, the busy one. Few of us can find time to be like Mary, the one who slows down and listens to Jesus.

The Church reminds us that our time is indeed limited and that it must be spent well. When we examine our conscience, we need to ask ourselves how much time we give to others. The Church wants us to put things into perspective as we journey through the days that remain to us on this earth.

We are all given a certain amount of time here. Our purpose is to become more deeply human. God will take care of the divine part. To be deeply human is to be part of this world with its imperfections and sorrows. We are asked to share our lives – and especially our time – with others. My neighbour on this earth is the one who needs me *now*.

When we observe people among us who seem to be acutely aware of the need of others and who go out of their way to help them, we know that the Kingdom of God is in our midst. Some people think that we live in terrible times. This is only part of the story. We live in wonderful times with saints and prophets among us.

It is the simple things that we do that advance the Kingdom among us – the phone call to a friend or relative who is housebound; the patient, compassionate listening to someone in pain; the act of kindness toward a stranger. These are the things that make our days on earth worthwhile, and cause the Lord to say to us, "You are not far from the Kingdom of Heaven."

God's Individual Care

Every year when I go to the St. John's Regatta, I think of what my uncle would say about the size of the crowd: "They say that you will find your loved ones in heaven … I can't even find someone at the Regatta."

My uncle has since passed on, and I am sure that the Lord has shed light on his theological problem. Yet my uncle's comments prompted me to reflect on how God could care for billions of people individually. The answer came to me in a quotation from Father Leo Trese, an American writer.

> God does not lose sight of us, as you or I might lose sight of one drop of water in the vastness of the ocean. Because of His Infinity, numbers mean nothing to God.

> If you were the sole survivor in an atomic war, God could not love you more personally than He does. At every moment, you have His complete attention, His undivided love. At this very instant, God is thinking of you, looking at you directly, loving you.

He is intensely aware of your present problem. He cares tremendously about what happens to you. Out of your present burden, imposed by the ignorance or malice of others (or your own foolishness) God is going to bring good to you.

I especially like the part about "your own foolishness." So many of our problems are not really problems at all but situations caused by our own foolishness. So many times we are our own worst enemies. We have not learned to love and value ourselves. Father Trese tells us something that we need to hear over and over again – we are valuable because we are loved by God.

Father Trese also addresses my late uncle's comments about size or numbers when he says, "because of His Infinity, numbers mean nothing to God."

All our experience has been with finite things – with people who are limited. People can only do so much and can only know so much, but with God there are no limits. There can be billions of people in the world, but "every moment you have His complete attention." Purely human thinking can never bring us to understand these facts. We must go beyond our limited human knowledge and move into the world of faith. Reality is not the sum of our perceptions.

If we rely only on human thinking uninspired by faith, we will believe that God is too busy to have much time to spend with us, that God is like an important official and that it is difficult to get an "audience" with him.

The truth is that "in him we live and move and have our being." God is at the very centre of our being, even when we are least aware of his presence and are sure that he has gone away.

Names

"What's in a name?" asks Shakespeare. Everything. A long time ago, my father told me I should always take the utmost care in getting people's names right. "Their name is the most important thing they have," he would say. "Find out what someone's name is; remember it and spell it correctly." In a real sense, my name is myself. I take pride in it and am happy when people call me by name.

Remember Zacchaeus, the man in the gospel who climbed the tree to see Jesus? Jesus did not say, "Hey, buddy, come down" or "You up there, come down and talk to me." He called Zacchaeus by name, thus honouring him.

It is embarrassing to forget the names of people we should know. Sometimes when we spot someone walking up to us we mutter to our partner, "Who is that?" We want to be armed with the person's name when we greet them.

Little people are just as important as big people when it comes to names. Caring people will always remember the names of little children and call the children by name when they meet them.

Names are important in the Bible, too. In the Psalms, God says, "I have called you by name." When Moses was trying to find out more about God, he asked God, "What is your name?" When Jesus gave Simon new responsibilities over the Christian community, he gave him a new name: Peter. When we have grasped someone's name we have somehow grasped the essence of that person.

I have kept in mind what my father said to me about the importance of names. Still, if I run into you and can't remember your name, forgive me. I am getting old.

Living Our Faith

When I was a child I got a very high mark in a religion test and was awarded a pair of wall plaques of Jesus and Mary. I received praise from family and friends and felt rather smug about my achievement. Later I read Cardinal John Henry Newman, who wrote, "Education produces the gentleman, not the saint."

My high mark in religion did not necessarily mean that I was a particularly religious or holy person, just that I had a good memory. Getting the highest mark did not mean I was the best person in the class.

Yet too often we focus on the intellect rather than on "goodness of life" or faithfulness to Jesus.

Knowing and doing are two entirely different things. St. Paul says he often knows what he should do, but does the opposite. We are the same. Sometimes we go against our inner voice and are led astray.

The truth is that religion is "caught," not taught. We learn about our faith through watching others. Parents today think they can't teach their children about the faith because they don't know everything about the subject. But children learn best through example. If parents are kind and loving to them and to others, the children have learned a Christian lesson for life. If children see parents welcoming strangers and helping them to feel at home, they are learning about the welcoming of Christ.

Parents are their children's first teachers in faith, and living examples of love. No need to panic. A little reading and a little adult education will help young parents steer their little ones on the right path.

It is helpful to read and think about God. But our relationship to God in prayer and our loving actions towards others are important signs that we are truly living our faith.

Friendship

It has been said that we have many acquaintances but few friends. If we were to make a list of all the people we know well enough to greet on the street, the list would probably be a long one. Most of us encounter hundreds and even thousands of people as we move through life. We probably know these people by name along with one or two facts about them, such as their occupation and marital status. We also know people through our work or through our children. A smaller group forms our social circle.

But how many really close friends do we have? How many people earn our trust and even our intimacy? When you come to think of it, there are likely no more than three or four people in the world whom you would consider to be your closest friends.

One of these special persons might be a spouse, a lifelong friend or a spiritual adviser whom we have been lucky enough to discover. From time to time we all need to confide in some trusted person, especially in situations that we feel we cannot handle alone. Our journey through life is the story of our need for each other.

Although we all need close friends, there are an awful lot of lonely people in our midst. Husbands and wives die; lifelong friends move away. Sometimes close friends betray our trust, and a once warm friendship turns to ashes. When these things happen, we feel very alone.

But Jesus stays with us. Storms may pass through our lives and we ourselves may change, but our Lord never changes. Jesus is a lifelong friend and brother.

Asking Questions

There are people who listen when you speak, and people who don't. There are also people who ask questions and people who don't. Not long ago I met a former high school classmate whom I had not seen for several decades. When I asked him what he had been doing for the past 30 years, he proceeded to give me a play-by-play of his major and minor achievements since I last saw him. The rest of the conversation revolved around him. I listened attentively, but I was more the audience than a companion or fellow communicator. I asked him several questions about himself and he answered each one in great detail. We parted with a handshake. Later it occurred to me that he had not asked me a single question about myself. I can give a complete report on his life, but he learned little or nothing about me.

Later I was reading a book by John Bradshaw on human relationships. Bradshaw deals with the issue of asking questions and relates it to the issue of creativity. He says that the greatest power we have is creativity. Creativity is based on the premise that we don't know everything. We are in a state of wonder. We go into the world to find things out by asking questions.

People who think they know it all feel no need to ask questions. This cuts them off from all kinds of new information and severely limits their horizons. People who are totally preoccupied with themselves will not take the time or the trouble to draw people out and get them talking about themselves. By asking questions we get people involved and at the same time we get them out of themselves.

Creative people can make connections between people. Two business acquaintances may have known each other for years; until you ask them where they are from, they may not realize that they grew up in the same neighbourhood, have similar backgrounds or many things in common.

Besides asking questions to get new information, we ask questions to involve people. To ask a person a question is to show that you value that person. It shows that you can be more complete by accepting what that person has to offer to you. It is an invitation for that person to participate in your life. It is an act of love and acceptance. On the other hand, never to ask a question is to demonstrate indifference.

To share communication with another, we must be willing to do two things: listen and ask questions. A careful reading of the gospels shows that Jesus was an excellent listener. He also asked a lot of questions. He made people feel important because they are important. We must be deeply committed to the belief that everyone we talk to is very important. Listen… and ask questions.

How God Speaks

"No one has ever seen God," St. John says in the first chapter of his gospel. Children must wonder why they never see God. They may hear their parents talk about God and may learn to pray, but where is God? What does he look like? What does he think about?

Theologians sometimes talk about the silence of God. Did God wind up the world and then walk away, or is he somehow involved in human activities? Just how silent is God? Does he speak? In what ways?

That question is answered for us in the first Letter to the Hebrews. St. Paul writes, "In old days, God spoke to our fathers in many ways and by many means, through the prophets; now at last in these times he has spoken to us, with a Son to speak for him."

What were the many ways in which God spoke to men and women in ancient times? One way was through nature. On a starry night, the Psalmist was so inspired by God's presence that he wrote,

"When I look at the sky which you have made, at the moon and the stars which you set in their place – what is man, that you think of him; mere man that you care for him?"

God also speaks through the prophets – ordinary people who were God's messengers. Many of them were very shy and physically unimpressive; and some had speech impediments. Oftentimes they were scared stiff of their task to speak on behalf of God, and tried to run away from their duties. The prophets prepared the way for the Word made flesh – Jesus.

The arrival of Jesus brings us closer to God. "Whoever has seen me has seen the Father," said Jesus. When Jesus speaks, God speaks.

To find out what God is like, prayerfully reading the New Testament is a good place to start. God became man in Jesus so that the silence and distance of God could give way to the flesh and blood humanity of Jesus. Jesus is for everyone. You don't need to be a theologian to call upon his name. God speaks to the simple and to the humble and to all those who sincerely seek Him. His Word is always with us. His Word is Jesus.

Doing Nothing

When is the last time you did absolutely nothing and did not feel guilty about it? One of the hardest things to do is – nothing. We find it so hard to do nothing. When people ask us, we will say we are doing something. "I am reading." "I am watching the ball game." "I'm admiring the sunset."

Yet some of the oldest writings about prayer tell us that if we wish to find God through prayer, we must learn to do nothing. In order to pray well, we must learn to simply *be*. Sit still and do nothing – don't even think.

Father Basil Pennington, in his book *Centering Prayer*, refers to the early Christian hermits and to the author of *The Cloud of Unknowing*, who teach that we must even lay aside all thoughts of God and simply be in his presence. God will do the rest. We are to rest peacefully in God's presence like a child in the arms of their father and simply be with him.

Our society has not conditioned us to behave this way. For people in our times who are continually plugged in to a dozen information sources every day, the idea of doing nothing is close to absurd. Yet if we are earnest about seeking God in this life, we must seek him in stillness.

Our Common Suffering

When asked about the major themes in his popular films, comedian and filmmaker Woody Allen has replied, "What I am trying to say is that we are all going through the same suffering."

What is this suffering that we are all going through? It is not an easily observable, highly focused suffering, like the death of a loved one or a serious illness. It is the suffering that comes with the knowledge that we are all imperfect beings and that we live in an imperfect world. The mere state of being human and imperfect, with desires that will never be fulfilled in this life, is a form of suffering that we all carry. This incompleteness is the basis of our search for God and for a perfect state of existence.

Our common suffering can lead us in two possible directions. It can lead us to bitterness and despair, or it can lead us to compassion and hope.

In his book *Power and Innocence*, psychiatrist Rollo May says that compassion is "the name of that form of love which is based on our knowing and our understanding each other." Since Christ knows and understands us, he is filled with compassion. Rollo May continues, "Compassion is the awareness that we are all in the same boat and that we all shall either sink or swim together. Compassion is felt towards another as much because he doesn't fulfill his potentialities – in other words, he is human, like you and me, forever engaged in the struggle between fulfillment and non-fulfillment."

An ancient early Roman expression says, "At the heart of man there is tears." The New Testament tells us that Christ will dry every tear and bring fulfillment to our human desires.

Christianity makes comedy possible. It is pretty hard to laugh about death if we see no future for us beyond the grave. Only the person with hope and compassion can laugh and dance and celebrate this earthly life, which is a prelude to eternal life.

If every man and every woman is my brother and my sister, it is because we share a common suffering in being together in this imperfect world. But it doesn't end there. Since Christ shares our human condition, we all share a common destiny in and through Him. We share hope and fulfillment in God.

Making Contact

In his book *Love and Friendship*, Allan Bloom writes, "Isolation, a sense of lack of profound contact with other human beings, seems to be the disease of our times."

Many factors in society tend to isolate us from each other. Young people leave their small communities and move to larger urban areas. More people work outside the home than they used to. People no longer visit each other's houses as freely as in the past.

Television dominates the home: many families sit in silence in front of the TV, speaking only during commercials.

How much of our contact with other people is profound? Half the time we talk about the weather or our favourite sports team. We ask people how they are, but have little interest in their answer.

Many people have become isolated even within the intimacy of their marriage. Judging from the wasteland of ruined marriages, there is a lack of profound contact between husbands and wives. This isolation is passed on to their children, many of whom no longer know just where they fit into the family and the world.

With the speed of modern life and the constant need to keep the wolf from the door, people seem to have little time for spiritual things. At the same time, there is a longing for significant encounters with others and a great need to feel part of a community. People desperately want to feel that they belong to something bigger than themselves. Many are turning away from materialism and focusing on family, relationships, community and the spiritual.

In moving toward a richer spiritual life, we will take the time to make profound contact with the people in our communities. We will break away from the isolationism that comes as a direct result of pursuing material wealth, with thoughts only of acquiring more and more for ourselves. We will regain a sense of the sacredness of the universe, human life and God.

Listening Up

Most people are all too happy to give us advice, but few indeed are willing to listen to our problems.

Some time ago in the United States, a man who worked as a mechanic and taxi driver put an ad in the paper. In the ad he offered to listen – simply listen – to anyone who needed to talk. For this service he would charge five dollars for 30 minutes. Needless to say he got lots of business. Some of his clients were from the higher economic bracket. One of his clients had bought an expensive home. He wanted to put a clothesline in his garden but found it difficult to act against the wishes of his neighbours. He wanted to talk about this problem, but felt that nobody would listen to him. The man who put the ad in the paper found that all kinds of people wanted to talk about all kinds of things. Business was very good because people had a terrific need to be listened to.

In his book *Loving Each Other*, Leo Buscaglia quotes a poem by an anonymous writer. The poem is called "Listen":

When I ask you to listen to me and you start giving advice you have not done what I asked.

When I ask you to listen to me and you begin to tell me why I shouldn't feel that way, you are trampling on my feelings.

When I ask you to listen to me and you feel that you have to do something to solve my problems, you have failed me, strange as it may seem.

Perhaps that is why prayer works for some people. Because God is mute and He doesn't offer advice or try to fix things. He just listens and trusts you to work it out for yourself.

So please, just listen and hear me. And if you want to talk, wait a few minutes for your turn and I promise I'll listen to you.

The kind of listening that we are talking about here is concerned and critical listening. We really hear what the other person is saying or trying to say. You become totally present to them. This kind of listening is not easy; it takes discipline. Most of us find it impossible to listen fully to what others say. The military has an expression it uses to get people's total attention: "Listen up."

As it says in the poem quoted above, people don't really want us to solve their problems. We couldn't do that even if we wanted to. People must solve their own problems, but sharing the problem with an attentive and critical listener can speed up the process.

Cosmos

Although God never changes, our concept of God is constantly evolving. Our understanding of our universe can help us to think about God with a greater sense of awe and wonder.

In ancient times, people pictured the world as a flat dish covered by a large dome, something like the Astrodome. There were gates or doors in the roof of the dome, which was surrounded by water. From time to time God would open the gates and let in some water. In dry seasons there was much praying and beseeching God to open the gates and send down some rain upon the earth.

Scientists today tell us that we are one of countless galaxies in an immense star system. Not long ago, a space vehicle that had been travelling for eleven years, sending signals back to Earth, left our solar system and moved into the great vastness beyond.

The more I am impressed and amazed by the vastness of the universe, the more I am in awe of the idea of a God who, unlike the universe, is infinite.

The writer of Psalm 8 used the visible universe to think about God. He wrote, "When I look at the sky, which you have made, at the moon and the stars, which you set in their places – what is man, that you think of him; mere man that you care for him?"

Reaching Out

Leo Buscaglia was a university professor in California. One year he noticed a very pretty girl sitting in his class. He never made a move to get to know her; he just noticed her. One day she wasn't there. He asked about her and was told the news. This young girl – beautiful, intelligent, only 20 years old – had committed suicide for no apparent reason. Leo Buscaglia changed his life after that incident. He realized that many people are starved for love. Many people live in terrible isolation. These people are not immediately recognizable. They may look happy and give the impression that they need no one, but they are desperately lonely.

Buscaglia began to study human love and the lack of it. He wrote many books about love and became a very powerful speaker on the subject. He points out that in our day-to-day activities we rarely, if ever, touch each other. We are often embarrassed to hug each other in appreciation, friendship or love.

There are many reasons why we don't embrace. Many of the reasons are cultural; some spring from our family background. Others spring from a fear of the touch being mistaken for something more sinister, as in the cases of teachers and students.

Whether we are the demonstrative type or more reserved by nature, we can still reach out to others and offer them both friendship and love. Leo Buscaglia felt that if he had gotten to know the young woman in his class, she might not have taken her own life. Many people who are silent before us are waiting for us to take the initiative and to offer them our friendship. Perhaps they simply do not have the confidence in themselves to make the first move. The responsibility, then, is ours.

The sign of peace in church is an invitation to us to reach out to others. This weekly sign reminds us to continually make the effort to reach beyond ourselves. This greeting points to a reality beyond itself: that we are here to care for and comfort each other. Since Christ lives in us, he continues to reach out to others in love through us.

Recognizing the Fat Lady

In *May We Borrow Your Husband?* Graham Greene writes, "There is no desire so deep as the simple desire for companionship." It rarely occurs to many Christians to apply the ordinary laws of life to their relationship with God. Perhaps this is why their worship of God is often incomplete. After 20 centuries of Christianity, too many Christians believe that there is but one way to reach God – the vertical approach.

In the vertical approach, God is "up there" and I am "down here." We talk to each other through prayer. Our relationship is really nobody's business but our own. Other people are in the way as I try to reach and commune with God. My salvation is really my own responsibility, and it is really everyone for themselves before God.

Jesus, on the other hand, seems to promote a horizontal approach when he talks about private prayer. In the horizontal approach, I see God when I look across. I see God when I look across the counter, across the street, across the dinner table, across the desk.

J.D. Salinger illustrates this point nicely in his book *Franny and Zooey*. Franny gets "hung up" trying to find God. Her brother Zooey tells her to do everything out of love for some imaginary "Fat Lady." He says that there is not anyone anywhere who isn't the Fat Lady. Then he says, "Don't you know who that Fat Lady really is? It's Christ Himself, Christ Himself, buddy."

The German theologian Bernard Haring puts it this way. "It is in communion with men, not in a selfish, individualistic approach to an eternal reward, that man finds God."

To really care, to be a true companion to someone in need, is to speed up the work of the salvation of the world. The mark of Christ's disciples is that they love one another. A Christian who does not care for others is a monster.

Christ's final judgment upon us reads like this: "Whatever you did to the least of my brothers and sisters, you did to me."

Stories and Scars

All of us have stories. All of us have scars. For the most part, we do not know each other's stories and we cannot see each other's scars.

How many people do we get close to in our lifetimes? How many people know our stories? How many people have seen our scars? Most of the time we protect ourselves from the scrutiny of others. When people ask us how we are doing, we seldom tell the truth.

One of the things we fear most in revealing ourselves to others is the loss of privacy. Whom can we trust? If we reveal ourself to another, will that other person respect our confidence?

The most important thing in a relationship is not sex, as the modern world would have us believe, but friendship. Where can I find someone I can trust completely, who, after seeing all my faults and sins, can love me without reservation?

Some people, because they have experienced betrayal by a good friend, close in upon themselves and never open themselves to others again. The people who seem the most distant and unapproachable are often the most lonely. They long to draw near to others, but they are afraid.

Sometimes, when we make the first step toward a lonely person, we find that, as they tell us their story, we are filled with understanding and compassion for them. They are surprised that someone has listened to them and understood them.

We are all in the same boat. We all have a past; we all have hurts and scars. Nobody is perfect. Every now and then lights go on, hearts open up and we experience grace through each other. At times like this we are all close to God. God, who knows all our stories and scars, loves us totally and absolutely, no matter where we have been or in whatever state we find ourselves.

Knowing we are loved by God, we can reach out to people who are lonely, and share God's love with them, restoring hope and life to others and advancing the Kingdom of God here on earth.

The Perfect Family

Most of us would like to think that we come from a perfect family. What's more, we would like *others* to think that we come from a perfect family. None of us feels comfortable admitting to ourselves or to others that this is not the case. The idea of a perfect family is a myth; why do we cling to it?

After all, none of us is perfect. Our mothers and our fathers are not perfect. Our siblings are not perfect. When we marry, we have one imperfect person marrying another imperfect person. This means that life has its share of conflict, and this is normal.

Paintings of the Holy Family can seem misleading. They look too good to be true. Jesus did not live an idyllic existence on this earth. Mary suffered knowing what lay in store for him. Joseph struggled to accept the amazing events announced by the angel. Jesus vanished for three days when he was twelve. Think of the worry that this incident caused his parents. When we see tension and problems in the very family of Jesus, how can we expect to escape these things in our own families?

Dr. Scott Peck begins his book *The Road Less Traveled* with the words "Life is difficult." Most of us would agree with him. If we consider that we are all in the same boat and that life is difficult for all of us, we would be slow to judge each other.

One of the great things about Jesus was his compassion for people. He listened and understood. We are called to be like him.

God does not expect us to be perfect in this life. God does want us to spend less time focused on ourselves so we can pay more attention to the needs of others. This is a constant challenge for us as Christians.

Despite our imperfections, God looks upon us all with love, and sees that we are His creatures and that we are not perfect but "good."

Pray Easy

We have always been under the impression that we must "pray hard." I used to think, in my youth, that "praying hard" meant exerting a lot of energy while praying. Praying hard meant great strain. You became tense as if you were pushing against a wall or a door, trying to get somewhere. The experience was draining and exhausting. The model for this kind of prayer experience was Jesus in the Garden of Gethsemane. We felt that if we really pushed ourselves, God would be convinced to grant us our requests.

The prayer of Jesus in the garden was not typical of his prayer to his father. The first chapter of the Gospel of St. Mark describes the more common approach Jesus took: "Very early the next morning, long before daylight, Jesus got up and left the house. He went out of town to a lonely place, where he prayed." Rather than energy and agony, we sense peace and stillness.

This may be a new message for those of us who are from the old school of praying hard. A book on prayer by Father Richard J. Huelsman, S.J., advises us that "to begin a period of prayer, relax, and open yourself to His presence. Become conciously aware: He is near, and cares about you and what you are about to do."

To stimulate the mind and the heart, many writers recommend a thoughtful reading of the gospels or of some spiritual writer. Fr. Huelsman advises us to "slow down, read slowly, aloud if possible, pronouncing the words. Think about what you are reading – about each sentence – about words and phrases. For practice, try one word with each breath."

This kind of advice ties in with the Eastern style of meditation in which holy people attempt to slow down the processes of their body in order to be more in harmony with their inner selves. Deep breathing is suggested. We have yet to learn how to sit still and to await the Lord. When the body is in harmony with the soul, it is easier for the Lord to speak to us.

When I was young, we learned to pray by doing a lot of talking to God. We talked incessantly in our prayers. We prayed so "hard," we heard only the sound of our own voice. We did not learn how to pray "easy."

Archbishop Alban Goodier reminds us that no matter what reading we do, we can never find Jesus as graphically as we will by reading the gospels themselves. In Goodier's words, the gospels allow us to "form a perfect picture" of Jesus. They give us "a living reality, the study of which will occupy us all of our lives, and even at the end the mind will not be exhausted."

Saving Things "for Good"

Many of us have a great habit of savings things "for good." Certain dishes and cutlery are to be used only for special occasions. The living room is to be used only for special company – the rest of the time it acts as a family museum.

I recently read of a young woman whose sister died suddenly. In going through her sister's things in preparation for the burial, she came across a beautiful and very expensive silk slip. The slip was still wrapped in tissue paper from the store. "She bought it six years ago," said her husband, "but she was saving it for good."

This incident touched the young woman deeply. She resolved to change her attitude toward life ... and death. She said, "I will spend more time reading and less time dusting. More time sitting on the deck admiring the view without worrying about the weeds. More time with family and friends and less time with committee meetings. I will use my good china to celebrate losing a pound. I will wear my best clothes and perfume going shopping and going to the bank. No more will I use the words 'someday' or 'one of these days.'"

Sometimes we wait too long to tell people that we love them. We somehow assume that they will be around forever.

Sometimes we seem to value our houses more than we do our children and their friends. We are afraid that kids will mark the floor or leave a few scrapes on the walls of the rec room. Isn't it better to welcome our children's friends and enjoy remembering their time with us than to have spotless walls to look at when we are old?

Our possessions, whether we have a lot or a little, are for our use. We should use them for ourselves, for our friends and, when we are able, for others who are in need ... but we should use them.

The aim of the Christian life is to live in a loving, caring community, not in a museum where we stand guard over treasures that we never use.

The man in the parable who was given one talent by the Lord, put the talent away and saved it "for good." It turned out to be for nobody's good – not even his own.

We all have gifts that other people need. When we come to realize this fact and attempt to share these gifts with others, we will be less lonely.

Everything we have is a gift from God. Everything we have is for good. Don't wait. Enjoy the good things that you have and share them with your brothers and sisters.

Moods

If we could control our moods by setting a button, most of us would probably set the button at "relaxed and happy" and leave it there for a lifetime. Unfortunately, we don't have that kind of control. Sometimes the relaxed feeling gives way to anxiety, tension, sadness, depression, fear or panic. We all experience a variety of moods, some of which are triggered by past experiences that are no longer in our conscious memory.

Sometimes we feel that we are unjustly victimized by our moods. "Don't talk to me today," we say. "I am in a terrible mood." "Catch the boss in a good mood," we say, "then ask him for a raise." From time to time we wonder, "Who is in charge here – me or my moods?"

The good news is that I am not my moods. I am not depression. I am not sadness or fear or even happiness – I am me. If I am down and depressed today, I will be happy and light-hearted again soon. This present mood is not all of my life.

The problem is that the media tell me I should be happy all the time. If I am not happy all the time, then something must be wrong with me. I am out of step with the world.

Many years ago, St. Thomas à Kempis wrote in *The Imitation of Christ* that "to have no pain or sorrow either of mind or of body is a state not of this world but of the next." A certain vague dissatisfaction with life, and a suspicion that there must be more to life, are signs that our souls are longing for heaven, the perfection of life.

God gives us internal resources and good friends to help us through difficult times. We often help each other in life without knowing it. On an evening when I feel light and happy I tell jokes to my friend and make him laugh. Later I learn that he was experiencing a crisis at work or at home and that my foolishness may have saved his sanity. On another occasion he will do the same for me.

We live with our moods and with the moods of others in the knowledge that Jesus, who experienced all human moods in his lifetime and who has been down the road before us, is waiting at the end of all our roads and all our moods to bring us to his Father's house, where all moods are transformed into joy.

Baptism and Mission

To be honest, I have not spent much time thinking about my baptism. Have you? I used to think
of baptism as a form of identification from the
Church. It allowed me to put "Roman Catholic"
next to my name when I filled out forms. Baptism
was something that took place in the distant past
and did not influence my present actions. It was as
if I had been spiritually branded with an indelible
mark, as we learned in school. I could not see this
mark, nor could anyone else.

The Second Vatican Council (1962–65) urged us
to take a deeper look at this issue. After describ-
ing the role of the clergy in *Lumen Gentium*, the
council went on to say, "less defined but *equally
important* is the role of the laity. Here we include
all the baptized members of the Church. The role
of the layperson is to consecrate the entire world.
More specifically, the laity are entrusted with the
important job of ordering the world's goods, so that
all people are cared for and no one is overlooked."

As baptized persons, we all have the obligation to
work with and for others – particularly the less

fortunate members of our society, such as the sick, the lonely, the grieving and recent immigrants and new Canadians. There is a great deal more to being a Catholic than simply attending Mass on Sunday.

Lumen Gentium adds, "Lay people live in ordinary circumstances of family and social life which is where they are called by God to give witness to the Light of Christ .... Thus lay people have the obligation to constantly develop a more profound grasp of their Christian faith."

Education never ends. We learn till we die. Many changes have been made in the way things are done in the Church in recent years. We can learn more about these changes through books, magazines, lectures and church websites.

Change is part of our lives. Living, as we do, in the 21st century, we no longer drive cars made in the 1930s and '40s. We drive modern cars. The Church, in bringing the good news of Jesus to the world, attempts to do so in ways that modern people will understand, while remaining true to the message of Jesus.

Hearing Our Stories

When I was a small child I believed that all my parents' friends were "old people." Old people were all those people who were older than me. I remember my uncle George saying one time, "There are no old people any more! They all used to wear black so you knew who they were – now they wear everything."

I see this as an improvement. By condemning older people to wear black as a kind of uniform, we were casting them off by themselves and making them fit a stereotype.

As I grow older, I spend more time thinking about old age. There is nothing magic about old age. Our faces and our bodies look older to others, but the thing that makes me myself remains the same.

There is a myth about old age that says that our personalities all change and we become someone else – namely, an old person. If we could maintain our health all throughout our lives, we would notice very little change in ourselves.

When we see or visit elderly people in nursing homes, we may forget that they have had rich, full lives. For an elderly woman lying in her bed, her story is very important; it has forged her identity.

She was once a young girl who went to her first dance, felt the thrill of her first kiss or the pain of a boyfriend who drifted away. She, like me, is on a journey. Her earthly journey is nearing its end, and the Lord, who has loved her all her life, will soon bring it to completion.

People say that they find it hard to visit old people. They don't realize how valuable to ourselves it is to listen to their stories. Their stories tell us more about ourselves and can give a deeper meaning to our own stories.

The greatest thing we can do for older people is let them know that they are welcome – in our homes, at church, or in the larger community.

Some people who visit seniors wonder, "What will I say?" Yet it is more important to be at their side than to "say the right thing." This is not a time for words, but a time for presence. It is a time to "be" for others more than a time to "say" things to others.

In many cultures the aged are revered and respected. We have moved a long way from this ideal. Let us remember that everyone is important. Everyone's story is important. Our job is to listen and learn.

Prayer and the Dragon

St. Cyril of Jerusalem wrote, "The dragon sits by the side of the road, watching those who pass. Beware lest he devour you. We go to the Father of Souls, but it is necessary to pass by the dragon."

Whether one lived in the fourth century, like St. Cyril did, or one lives in the 21st century, as we do, the basic human journey remains the same. We spend a relatively short time in this world en route to another world that has no end. We are pilgrims on a journey. As Gail Sheehy suggests, we all go through various "passages" or critical points along the way. We must all "pass by the dragon."

The dragon is a symbol of the forces of darkness within ourselves or in the world around us. These include any influence in our lives that can sidetrack us on our journey toward God.

It may sound dramatic to talk of the forces of darkness within ourselves, but each of us instinctively knows what St. Paul is talking about when he writes to the Romans, "I don't do the good I want to do; instead, I do the evil that I do not want to do."

Even the best of us is filled with contradictions. We are pulled in many directions and fall short of our goals in countless ways. What can we do about this state of tension that is so much a part of the human condition?

In his book *The Second Journey: Spiritual Awareness and the Mid-Life Crisis*, Gerald O'Collins suggests that if we are to "pass by the dragon" that sits by the side of the road, we must "keep more than a rumor of prayer alive ... for the believing traveller, however, and perhaps even for the half-believer, prayer can deal with a felt loneliness and provide a strengthening assurance."

The message seems to be that prayer is important for anyone who wants to reach "the other side" safely. Perseverence in prayer will give light to our journey. It will also keep us out of the path of the dragon.

Knowing Others

We make a lot of assumptions about people based on their physical appearance. We like to look over new people and form an image of them in our minds. This image or concept is based largely on our own prejudices and at times distorted perceptions. We will never know what people are truly like until we talk to them.

Sometimes we miss out because we allow our feelings to govern our behaviour. A dull-looking fellow at a party turns out to be a fascinating person with important things to share with us. A carefree-looking girl who lives next door has a great sadness in her life that she is trying to cover up. A brash, tough-looking guy at work is insecure. People are not what we see. When we talk to people we give them the opportunity to reveal themselves to us.

A lot of people either cannot or do not want to reach out and communicate with others. But if you don't talk to people and tell them who you are, they will never know about you.

How can we know God? By talking to God and listening to him. God is a great mystery, but he reveals himself in many ways. One major way is through Jesus. When Jesus speaks, God speaks. The Bible tells us that God has spoken to us in many ways over the centuries; for Christians, the clearest way in which God speaks is through Jesus. If we want to find out what God is like, the gospels can shed much light on the subject.

Many of us grew up learning about a very abstract kind of God. God may have seemed like a stranger to us. Through the stories, thoughts and actions of a real historical person – Jesus – we learn new things about God. God is a loving and merciful parent, like the forgiving father in the parable of the prodigal son.

The false image we might have of God is very much like the false image we create about a stranger we meet at a party. Our ideas spring more from our imagination than from reality. When we talk to people and let them talk to us, we see the real person who is before us. Similarly, by our prayerful reading of the gospel, we free ourselves from our false images of God and find peace and happiness as God's true friends.

Knowing How Others Feel

We often assume that we know what other people are going through. To show our concern, we tell our friends, "I know exactly how you feel." It is comforting to think that we can help someone by our empathy and understanding.

Yet can we truly be sure of what another person feels? We may try our best to feel for the other person, but our perception will always be that of an outsider.

Although this is true of people, no such gap exists between us and God. God knows what we feel because God became one of us. Jesus knows what it is to be both God and human. God *does* know and understand how we feel. The terrors of being alone, of being the only traveller on the road, have been lightened or taken away.

In taking on human nature, God is not play-acting at being human. The man Jesus is truly involved in everything human, except sin. God eats with sinners. God is hungry, thirsty and terrified about the suffering he must face at the end of his life on earth.

We could spend the rest of our lives meditating on the words "The Word became flesh."

People who risk themselves and reach out to others in a sense become for a short time the "flesh" of the other person. Like God, they take on all the joys and risks that this involves. We are free either to show compassion or to remain safely aloof. Jesus has come among us to urge us to choose the route of compassion and incarnation.

Dis-incarnation

Where is everybody? In this so-called age of information, it seems that everybody is out. We are invited to leave a message. We feel like a fool as we pour out our hearts into voice mail. Our high-tech communications systems have made it harder to reach out to other human beings. Some people screen calls to further limit contact with others.

Talking to people to get information is a thing of the past. How do I find out if my friend's flight is on time? I am mystically transported by computer to Toronto or Montreal or Halifax and asked to go through a maze of choices to get to the simple piece of information I seek. Somewhere along the line I fall off the ladder, hang up in frustration and head for the airport to see if my friend is there.

Marshall McLuhan saw an irony in the fact that, whereas in the Incarnation, the Word became flesh, in the modern age the flesh has been separated from the word. We see evidence of people, but we cannot find them. Companies have placed electronic mazes around themselves, and we need to be resourceful to reach the people inside.

In a word, our world has become very impersonal.

What is the role of the Christian in such a world? We have to work harder to make our world a human place in which to live. There is a lot more to life than computers, technology and information. Technology, in encouraging distance between people, can cause us to overlook some of our obligations as Christians. Mother Teresa's message was so simple: observe people, see their needs, and do what you can to help them. Jesus tells us the same thing. This message overrides technology and urges us to look at what is really important in life.

Something very important is being lost in this impersonal world. We want to connect with others so that we can have travelling companions on our one-time journey through this life. Loneliness seems to increase as communication systems proliferate. By choosing to communicate with each other and with God, we see technology as a tool, but not the guiding force in our lives.

The Mystery of Evil

Many adventure novels have to do with the Nazi era. A popular theme is that of the Jewish Nazi hunter who combs the world looking for aging war criminals. Occasionally he finds one living in quiet comfort in Argentina or Brazil, and sets his mind to bringing the criminal to justice. The theme is a fascinating one: it reminds us that evil is a continuing reality in the world. It also points to the fact that there is an opposing force that seeks justice.

There are more recent images of evil for our consideration. The names of Idi Amin and Pol Pot invoke fear in many hearts; the terroist attacks on the World Trade Center in New York City in 2001 are still impossible to comprehend. No one has ever really understood why evil exists, but the answer is closely tied to our freedom to act upon our environment and to shape the events of human history.

Human beings remain incomplete, imperfect. We struggle with evil and turn our backs on God.

Christ understood this problem. He knew what was in our hearts. Human evil brought him to the horror and darkness of the cross. Yet through the cross he brought about the light that can overcome the darkness. Good and evil will co-exist side by side till the end of the world. We will see a lot of both of these realities in our own lifetime. Our own freedom of choice will ultimately determine whether we are on the side of light or of darkness.

Pigeonholing People
We Meet

We generally think of prejudice as relating to race or culture or social background. But prejudice runs much deeper even than this.

We all have a tendency to pigeonhole people. When we meet someone for the first time, we find a word to describe that person to ourselves. We feel we know them. The person must fit into one of our categories.

The tendency to play God is a strong one for us. We love to pass judgment on others and we feel so proud when we turn out to be right.

We don't seem to realize that it is ridiculous to identify a person by one characteristic – positive or negative. Until I take the time to truly get to know someone, they remain one-dimensional. The same is true for me.

To the waitress in a restaurant I might be "the pork chops." To a cab driver I might be "the fare to Mount Pearl." But when I begin to talk to the waitress or the cab driver, asking about their day or their interests and sharing mine, something of "me" begins to register with them. At the same time, they become for me fellow members of the human race.

Like Jesus, we have to give every man and woman a chance to tell us who they are. Jesus spoke to a woman at Jacob's well. To the disciples she was a "Samaritan." To Jesus she was an unfortunate girl with a problem past. The disciples did not save her or make her a better person by pigeonholing her. Jesus changed her life because he got to know and accept her.

There is only one person in the world upon whom I can rightly pass judgment: myself. The irony is that while we are quick to judge others, many of us have never made an honest, realistic judgment of ourselves.

Christ warns us about passing judgment on others. He warns us about pigeonholing people. The person who thinks that they know everybody may end up not knowing anyone.

Forgiveness

Anger and bitterness have a way of chipping away at our health. We are all aware of family feuds and resentments that prevent brother from speaking to brother and daughter speaking to mother. Some of those rifts are lifelong. How much of life is lost by those who cannot find it in their hearts to forgive? Forgiveness leads to freedom.

Father Patrick Ryan, S.J., said, "All of us have been forgiven an enormous debt. As forgiven people, we need to forgive. Wrath held on to tenaciously only destroys the wrathful."

Forgiving those who have injured us in the past is not easy. Some people are fortunate enough to resolve their inner conflicts and become free. Others are tortured all their lives, haunted by ghosts from the past. God forgives all when we truly regret our actions. These people need God's grace as well as loving friends and professional counsellors to break with the past.

In the New Testament, Jesus tells us about the master who forgave his servant a very great debt only to discover that this same servant dealt harshly with another servant who owed him money.

As a forgiven people we are expected to forgive. Failure to forgive holds its own punishment: loneliness, alienation and just plain missing out on a lot of life.

Some people who have been bitter for years have experienced a conversion due to the prayers of their friends and the working of the Holy Spirit. Others persist in their unhappy state.

If we have friends who turn bitter or become alienated from society, we must not give up on them. They need to see the forgiveness of Christ in people like us.

Success

Bookstore shelves groan under the weight of books on "success." How to succeed in business ... in marriage, in the kitchen, in the bedroom, at work, as a host, as a parent, as a working mother, as a stock market investor – these are the issues that occupy people today. Our society is divided largely along economic lines. The rich rarely encounter the poor. The poor rarely encounter the rich. The middle class often has pretensions about being associated with the rich. The poor are mostly left out in the cold.

A few years ago I found myself in the middle of a modern parable as I drove down the street. A well-known, highly successful local businessman was driving a Jaguar with all the bells and whistles. I was behind him in my old Toyota. Then a thought struck me. We were both on the same road! The rich man did not have his own road. We came to a red light. The Jaguar stopped for the light. We were both governed by the same rules!

Have you observed that when you meet someone new, they do not ask you who you *are*? They always ask what you *do*. They want to know your position in society. We are largely defined by what we do. If I have a title or a big job, then I am worthy of attention. If I am nobody special I am easily ignored.

Jesus upset a lot of people when he said that everyone is special; everyone is important. To live as a Christian is to ignore wealth and position and to see ourselves as a group of brothers and sisters on the same road, heading for the same destination. God asks us to show compassion and mercy and love to all.

TV and newspapers are full of bad news. We all need to learn about the Good News. The bad news of Good Friday gives way to the Good News of Easter Sunday. We are all called to live out the Good News of Jesus every day of the year. Without the resurrection, despair and hopelessness would prevail.

Jesus offers us the success that we can never attain by ourselves. The victory has been won. As Mother Teresa used to say, "We don't have to be successful, we just have to be faithful."

Life After Retirement

Many people are afraid to retire. They think that life ends when their career or job ends. When I used to think about retirement, I pictured myself on a foggy, rainy day looking out the window of my home in a state of depression. Retirement was a fearful concept.

Now that I am retired, I have a much more positive view of the matter. The possibilities for getting involved in the community after retirement are endless. It is a question of figuring out what your favourite volunteer activities are and identifying something that you want to do. There is also a lot more time for reading and reflection than ever before. Retirement is an exciting new phase in our lives. We have the time, once we are off the daily treadmill, to take stock of ourselves and our relationships to reflect on what God wants of us for the rest of our days.

Perhaps the greatest part of our life is yet to come. God's plan for us does not end when we turn 65. God may have been preparing us all our lives for some important work that only we can do once our formal work responsibilities are done. Cardinal Henry Newman strongly believed that every life has a purpose and that we might never know in this life what that purpose is. Yet it is very real to God.

If God has taken us to this particular point in our lives, you can be sure that he will bring our lives to completion according to his plan for us.

The most successful person in the world's eyes may be in great need in God's eyes. People who are seen as losers and failures in the world's eyes may be big winners in God's eyes.

The hunger for spirituality in the world is endless. The superficiality of our culture, as seen through popular TV shows and magazines, tells us nothing of our greatness or of our destiny. Many people today have lost sight of who they are; others have never known.

Retired people can give witness to God in the world in numerous ways. Our knowledge of the past can give the young the framework they need to make sense of the present. Our faith roots can help the young to understand the importance of having a relationship with God.

Our lives aren't over when we stop working. The day we retire could be the first day of the rest of our lives!

Spiritual Baggage

We all carry a certain amount of spiritual baggage.

For my generation, a prime example is what I call the "individual salvation syndrome." Romeo Maione, a social activist in the Catholic tradition, once said, "We are all on the big Christian train to heaven ... and to hell with everyone else."

Prayers were individual and private. In the past, public prayer was very impersonal. Keeping it impersonal emphasized that the most important thing was one's personal, private relationship with God. The main task of every Christian was to save your own soul. Other people entered into the picture only after you were sure that your own soul was being well taken care of. All in all, it was a very selfish kind of approach.

To this day I find spontaneous prayer with a group to be difficult. I feel exposed, as if people are focused on me and not on God. That's a kind of spiritual baggage.

Another negative aspect to our spirituality was a preoccupation with "sins of the flesh." Other, more serious offenses were overlooked in the search for sinful sexual thoughts or behaviour.

Father William O'Malley, S.J., writing in an April 1994 issue of *America*, says,

> Jesus was never quick to condemn the sexual sinner. In fact sexual sins did not seem very high on Jesus' priority list. Surely not as high as they have been in the eyes of the official church, owing to the intervention of Plato, St. Augustine and others. Great minds, but they were not Jesus. He was not as blasé about sin as many nominal Christians like to believe he was. But perhaps the root sin is that of having "an obtuse spirit," which is the narcissism which refuses to admit one did wrong and the inertia that finds it too much effort to go back to the first wrong turn and start over.

All of us carry some spiritual baggage. Sometimes this baggage separates us from other Christians and from Jesus. It's time to let go of that baggage and follow Jesus, carrying only what we wish to share with others.

Conscience and Convention

For the individual, the highest law is personal conscience. People who violate their own conscience to please others divide and destroy themselves. Truly courageous persons know that there may be no precedent to the major decisions they must make about themselves and their own lives; no one has lived their life before. That is why we are ultimately alone in our decision making.

Seeking advice is wise, and we would be fools to disregard the sound judgment of others, but in the end it is up to us. Much of life is a gamble. Will this career suit me? Shall I change my career now before I am too old to reshape myself for a new one? Shall I marry? Shall I marry this particular person? Shall we have a family? How large should our family be?

Some people are blessed with good, sound judgment. Many people make terrible mistakes of judgment and, in so doing, ruin their lives or someone else's. All of us try to escape the decisions forced upon us by conscience, from time to time, particularly if these decisions are painful and will hurt those close to us.

Sometimes our conscience may force us to make a move or take a stand that will place us outside our familiar culture and remove us from the acceptance of the group. The ability to move in defiance of one's culture or peer group when one's conscience is sure marks the person of courage and decision.

Each person must strive to know who he or she is and to have the courage to be that person no matter the cost. Most of us lack the courage to be true to ourselves; often, the price is too high. The socially and emotionally damaged in our society are those who have chosen convention before conscience.

Those who are untrue to their conscience are deeply unhappy people. They are people who have crawled all their lives when they might have run. Few people have what theologian Paul Tillich calls "the courage to be." The wonder of Jesus was that he believed in everything he did. He had the courage to be.

It does not matter, in the end, whether we were right or wrong. The important thing is that at every given moment of our lives, we tried to do what we thought was right and were willing to live with the consequences of our actions.

Pleasure and Joy

Some people give the impression that there is something wrong with us if we are not having fun all the time. These people would have us believe that life is about having fun and not much else. Illness and old age have no place in their thinking. People around the world who watch sitcoms on TV must believe that North American families are always laughing. Unless we are having fun all the time, we feel out of sync with society.

We even hide any unpleasant experiences from others – the trip that was a disappointment, the expensive purchase that was a waste of money, the child who is having difficulties. We tell people that we are feeling great and that everything is going well for us. Our Christmas letters mention only the good things that have happened over the past year, but not the struggles or pain.

Pleasure is a superficial and fleeting experience. Joy, on the other hand, is life-giving and lasting.

When we see people who are truly joyful, we want to know what they have going for them. Often it has nothing to do with money or health. Instead, it seems to be the ability to break out of their isolation and reach out to others. Those who develop genuine concern for others often attain joy. Those who remain trapped inside themselves will seek out pleasure, but rarely find joy.

In the first century of Christianity, people would look at the Christians and see their joy. They would say, "See how they love one another."

Jesus promised peace and joy to those who follow him, but offered no immunity from problems and sorrows. In an age of pleasure, we are encouraged to follow the prayer that says, "Let us put our hearts where true joy is found."

The Future

Many people spend so much time worrying about the future that they have no time left to live in the present. Somebody said to me the other day, "There is no such thing as the future ... it may never come. There is just *now*."

We spend a great deal of time worrying about things that may never happen. People get into a real frenzy worrying about diseases they may never have.

We simply cannot have complete control over our future. Jesus told the story of the foolish man who filled all his barns with grain, thinking he would live forever. As it turned out, he died that very evening. The future he worried about never came.

Henri Nouwen talks about those things that are "action" in our lives and those things that are "passion." The action part of our life is where we are in charge, where we determine our own life's direction. The passion refers to those parts of our lives over which we have no control.

Nouwen says, "Because most of my life is passion, things being done to me, only small parts of my life are determined by what I think, say or do. But the truth is that my passion is a much greater part of my life than my action." This statement is true for all of us. In this world, we are shaped by events more than we think. We do not select the time or place of our birth or of our death. We can practise healthy habits, but we cannot ward off sickness forever. Many elements in our lives are totally beyond our control.

Jesus urges us to leave the future in his hands. He reminds us of the birds of the air and the flowers of the field. They don't worry about the future, but our heavenly Father looks after them.

The great pity about worrying about the future is that we leave ourselves no time to enjoy the present. All we really have is now.

Father Anthony de Mello tells of a man condemned to death who sits in his prison cell in terror. Suddenly he asks himself, "When am I going to be executed?"

"Tomorrow," he answers.

Then, he says, "Tomorrow does not exist. I only have now. If tomorrow does not exist, why am I concerned about it?" So the man lies down and has a good night's sleep.

Tomorrow is in God's hands, not mine. My job in this life is to live to my highest potential *now*.

More Busy Than Bad

Father Ron Rolheiser, O.M.I., an excellent writer on spirituality, hits the nail on the head when he says in his book *The Holy Longing* that people these days are "more busy than bad, more distracted than non-spiritual, and more interested in the movie theatre, the sports stadium, and the shopping mall and the fantasy life they produce in us than we are in church. Pathological busyness, distraction and restlessness are major blocks today within our spiritual lives."

Why is it so difficult for us to sit and do nothing? Many people are so busy they say, "I never stop."

Why don't we ever stop? Are we afraid of what might happen to us if we did?

"Pathological busyness" is a good way to describe the person who constantly talks on their cell phone, checks their e-mail or is chained to their laptop. Never before have people been so busy ... or so it seems. This state of over-busyness is harmful to our spiritual lives. We have no time to be still.

We need some way to make our escape from this busy world every day, even for a short time, and to allow ourselves to do nothing. We should build quiet moments into our day, during which we can listen to God's voice within us.

Bookstores are filled with spiritual titles. Many of these books are presented in the format of short meditations, because people have no time to read long texts these days.

My approach is to bring a small book or magazine on spirituality with me wherever I go. During "wasted" moments – waiting in bank lines, at bus stops, at supermarket checkouts, waiting to see the doctor or the dentist, I read. I see bored faces in these lineups and waiting rooms. Few people seem to be enjoying these situations. We can use these times of waiting to learn about God and carry on our relationship with Jesus.

People can talk to God anytime and anywhere they want. Young parents can talk to God while tending a sick child or while making school lunches. Business people can talk to God as they drive from meeting to meeting. Sales staff can talk to God as they wait for customers to visit their store.

I once asked my mother how she prayed. She replied, "I don't know … I just talk to God." We can all do that … anytime, anyplace.

Saving the Earth

When we were growing up, we saw the world as a vast place with endless supplies of everything. The idea of running out of water or trees, for example, was absurd.

We now know that the world is but a tiny speck in an endless universe. My generation did not grow up with that wonderful picture of the world from outer space. Photographs taken from space have done a lot to place our world in perspective.

Now we realize that our world has only so much to give the six billion people who live on the planet. Scientists at the Massachusetts Institute of Technology tell us that we have enough water to last us for 20 or 30 years, that trees are being harvested faster than new ones can grow, and that smokestacks are churning out more pollutants than the atmosphere can handle. In 40 years there will be eleven billion people on earth: that spells catastrophe if present patterns continue.

Does all this have anything to do with religion? Doesn't religion have to do with the next life and not this one? The plight of our earth is indeed an issue for people of faith. A theology of ecology is emerging. We have a moral obligation to do our bit to preserve the earth.

The hopeful thing is that young people today are much more environmentally conscious than we were. They have grown up learning about how to care for the earth.

When we die, the world will pass on to our children and to our children's children. In the meantime, all people are called to be good stewards of the earth. God speaks to us through modern-day prophets who tell us to care for our home, the earth.

Impressions

A couple of years ago I had a visit from an old friend who is now living in the United States. We went over many old memories and told stories about the past. At one point my friend referred to a statement I had made to him many years earlier. He told me he had often thought about what I had said, and that my words had influenced his life. I was stunned: I didn't have the least recollection of saying this particular thing to him. At the time I had no way of knowing that my words would have had such a lasting effect.

Since that conversation with my friend, other people have mentioned that things they have said in casual conversation have been remembered for years and were sometimes acted upon. We don't realize the kind of impression we are making on people.

Even casual remarks can have a strong influence on others – we can say that every encounter we have with others is important. By observing us, people are learning about themselves and about God.

God uses each of us to influence each other. When we say that God speaks through people, we mean that God uses our family, our friends, our associates and even our enemies to get through to us.

Some people have a very low opinion of themselves. They think that they count for nothing, but that is not true. Every human being is a signpost pointing to God. Those who are helpless and suffering can stop us in our tracks and show us our total dependence on God, which we may have forgotten.

Every life is important. Every encounter we have with others has the potential to be a dynamic encounter with God.

As an old priest once said to me, "For the thousands of people that you have yet to meet in your life, you may be the only Christ they will ever know."

Masks People Wear

The world presents us with a great variety of people. Some are rich and healthy; others are rich and have some physical illness. Some are poor and healthy; others are poor and physically ill. Some seem to have everything in the way of money, talent and strength. Others appear to have nothing.

We all have the habit of comparing ourselves to others and sometimes wishing that we had the poise, the self-possession or the talent of another person. Things seem to come easily to certain people, while we have to work or fight or struggle to get by.

As we grow older, we come to know people better. One basic fact comes to our attention: every person wears a mask to hide their own pain. Beneath these masks we are basically alike. We all have one thing in common: our inner poverty. No matter how much wealth we may have, we are all poor before God. We all need his help and support.

When God said in the Bible, "Without me, you can do nothing," he was not writing heavenly poetry or passing on beautiful thoughts for us to read. He was throwing a realistic spotlight on our condition as men and women in this world. It is curious how we struggle to hide our weaknesses from others. There is a terror deep inside us that if another person sees our weakness, we will be rejected and cast aside. Yet experience teaches us that if we ever get the courage to tear away our mask and face people the way we really are, we are more accepted, trusted and even loved than when we hid behind the mask.

It is only when we find the courage to stop pretending to ourselves and to others how wonderful we are that we begin to see what God sees when he looks at us. The mystery of it all lies in the fact that God sees us as we really are – in our poverty and weakness – and loves us.

This, in essence, is what faith is all about. We become Godlike in this world when we see our own weakness and the weaknesses of others, and go on loving ourselves and others because God's love has given us worth.

Heaven is a place where our masks are checked at the door. In heaven everyone is himself or herself. And that is … heavenly!

The Disappearing Dinner Hour

Whatever happened to the family dinner? Families used to get together each evening to eat, tell stories and share the stuff of life. These gatherings helped family members, especially the young, to establish their identity and their roots.

Many questions or concerns got resolved at these family dinners. Through example, children learned much about the way to live a good Christian life. Problems were discussed and the young developed attitudes that would help them all through their lives.

Fast food, frozen dinners, television and text messaging have done much to destroy this important custom. With family members having different work and after-school schedules, the dinner table is often empty during the traditional supper hour.

Does this phenomenon have anything to do with living the Christian life? I think it does.

Eating together has been an important event for Christians since the beginning. St. Luke tells us that Jesus often joined his friends for dinner. The Mass itself was instituted during the Passover meal. It was at table that Jesus first offered his friends bread and wine as his own body and blood, and urged them to carry on this tradition "in memory of me."

There is a direct relationship between the table at home and the table at church. The priest faces the people because he is a dinner guest with us at the banquet. We gather at the table as a community.

Christianity is about community; yet many behave as if it involves only a private relationship with God. The Christian life invites us to eat and live together. The home is called the "domestic Church." Eating together at home is a sort of liturgy. Food is vital to our lives, but so is the togetherness that comes with the experience.

When our families gather to eat, the Spirit has much to tell us.

Choosing Happiness

I once read about a woman who was left paralyzed after a car accident. Her experience led her to reflect, "No one is born happy. Everyone makes their own happiness."

Happiness does not depend upon social status, education or health. Some people who have everything are desperately unhappy; others, who have little in the way of material possessions or opportunities, are happy.

Many people allow a consumer-centred society to decide for them when they are happy. According to the ads we see, one year we won't be happy without a certain type of computer. Another year, happiness consists in owning a particular MP3 player or video-game system.

The product that is supposed to bring happiness changes from year to year; the average person must work very hard to keep up with the demands of the pace-setters.

How do people who possess very little of this world's goods find happiness? Strange as it may seem, happiness is a personal decision.

The only person in the world who can make you happy is yourself. Similarly, the only person in the world who can make you unhappy is yourself. Showing gratitude each day for the simplest blessings – a place to live, food on the table, families who love us – reminds us how lucky we are. With these thoughts in mind, it becomes easier to be optimistic and to choose happiness.

We are free to choose the light or the darkness. We are the masters of our own happiness.

Healing

Jesus did a lot of healing during his three years of ministry. People from all walks of life, both Jews and Gentiles, were healed of their physical and mental illnesses. The only thing they had in common was their faith in the Lord.

The tradition of healing has always been part of our church.

When I was a young man, I had two experiences with this healing tradition. I spent a summer working at the Cap-de-la-Madeleine shrine as a tour guide. I met many people who had a variety of illnesses. I assumed that they were visiting the shrine to seek a cure for their illness, but this was not always the case. They came to the shrine to seek whatever help the Lord would give them, even if it meant the strength to live with their afflictions. While many people will not be cured of their symptoms, their souls can find healing.

Later, I accompanied about a hundred people, most of whom were disabled, to Fatima, Lourdes and Rome. Some of us were there to help the people with disabilities get from place to place and assist them when needed. While at first I felt guilty for being so healthy, I realized that my health was what allowed me to help these others. I soon learned that many of them were healthier in mind and spirit than those of us who were attending them! God had worked miracles, creating joy and beauty within them.

Some people think that miracles at these shrines involve the throwing away of crutches and other such dramatic events. A woman once asked us at Cap-de-la-Madeleine, "When is the next miracle?" The obvious answer is "God knows."

The real miracles were often internal. Sometimes they involved receiving the courage to live with an illness or to die in the peace of Christ, feeling loved and protected and knowing that one was truly going home to God.

The healing power of Jesus is very real and is prevalent in our society. Many people experience inner healing, but may not talk about it. Physical healings are taking place as well; some of them are miraculous.

We can feel free to pray to Jesus for healing, and even for a miracle. A close friend of mine is seriously ill. We are praying to the Lord for him. Our prayers are made in hope, knowing that Jesus reaches out and heals all those who come to him.

Harmful Concepts of God

When I was young, I thought you could go to hell forever for eating a hot dog on Friday. (I wondered if you could be condemned for eating only half a hot dog or even one bite.)

Another person I knew had a religious snowflake fetish. If she was walking to Mass in the early morning and a snowflake drifted into her mouth, she figured that she had broken her fast and could not receive communion. Then there was the lady who weighed her morning toast during Lent. Some people believe that it is better to visit a foreign shrine than to go to Mass at home ... and on it goes.

Foolish religious thinking must be offensive to God: it implies that God is just as foolish and as small as we are! Having a faulty concept of God in our minds can cause us to be unhappy all our lives. We used to believe that mortal sins were so easy to commit, we could be committing them without even knowing it.

In all of this, we really didn't give God much credit for having any sense. People have suffered a lot over the years because of such false thinking. Some will not go to communion unless they confess their sins before each Eucharist – even if they have no mortal sins to confess. Some used to sit through communion because they felt they were unworthy to receive. Others believed that Christians should be miserable all the time and find no enjoyment in life. If life was enjoyed, then there must be something wrong.

Jesus came to set us free, but we are often caught up in our own chains.

Children today learn about Jesus right from the start. This seems to be a natural way to learn about God's mercy and love. We old-timers started off with an abstract God whom we largely misunderstood.

In his own day, Jesus criticized people for following the letter of the law rather than its spirit. Many of us have fallen into the same trap. But we can change that. By focusing on the Good News of Jesus, we will have every reason to be joyful and thankful to God.

Love and Friendship

While I was reading *The Russia House* by John Le Carré, one line leapt out at me. Katya is asked about her relationship with her lover: "Do you like him – as well as love him? Does he make you laugh?"

Katya replies without humour, "I believe that without me he would break." Their relationship seems to be a deadly earnest one based on passion and dependency. It is a relationship doomed to failure. These people will never loosen up and laugh at each other. They will never become friends.

I remember years ago reading an article by Father Andrew Greeley in which he asked, "Is your wife a friend of yours?" Young engaged couples are very preoccupied with love and being in love. Sometimes not enough attention is paid to their friendship. A marriage partner has to be a friend for life; it is important to develop a close friendship early on in the relationship.

Our consumer society places a lot of pressure on young couples to focus on the wedding day rather than the marriage. The marriage preparation courses that are offered by the churches invite young couples to slow down, get off the roller coaster of wedding preparations and think about the rest of their lives. Even couples who go to these sessions reluctantly find the talks and discussions energizing and helpful.

Marriage is a lot to think about. It is very important to go beyond the passion and find out if you really like your partner. Can your relationship handle differences of opinion, financial pressures, in-laws, raising children and facing life's ups and downs?

Every divorce is a failure of friendship. Too many people get married without exploring their friend-ship, either before or after the wedding ceremony.

Dr. Scott Peck, in his bestselling book *The Road Less Traveled*, reminds us that love is not a feeling but a deliberate act of will in which we decide to commit ourselves to a particular person. This rela-tionship has to be one primarily of friendship. How can I live for 40 or 50 years with someone I do not like or who is not my friend? The best question of all to ask before marriage is the question asked of Katya: "Do you like him – as well as love him? Does he make you laugh?"

Marriage and Grace

It is said that about half of all marriages today end. This incredible statistic makes a strong statement about the times in which we live.

One of the biggest problems facing marriages today is stress. It is becoming harder and harder to make a decent living and to bring up children properly in a world that seems to be falling apart.

The casualties of broken marriages are all around us. Single-parent families are on the rise. Single moms and dads burn themselves out trying to provide the necessities of life and spend enough time with their children.

Where can families find direction today? Whom can they turn to? There is a greater need for religion and spirituality in families today than ever before.

Our problems are too complex for us to solve on our own. We need God's help to survive. God speaks directly to all married couples through St. Paul (Romans 12) in one of the suggested readings for the marriage Mass.

Paul tells us that there are five things that we must do to have a blessed and happy marriage.

1. "Do not model yourself on the behaviour of the world around you." You don't need a big house or the latest MP3 player to be happy. Don't let your happiness depend on having all the things that society promotes.

2. "Have a profound respect for each other." Marriages cannot survive without mutual respect. The high incidence of abused women is a warning sign to society that this respect is often lacking.

3. "Do not give up if trials come." A society that is used to instant rewards will not tolerate the "trials" of marriage. We have to accept the suffering that often comes with marriage and family life, and not give up when the magic of a relationship seems to wear off.

4. "Keep on praying." The old saying is still true: "The family that prays together, stays together."

5. "Treat everyone with equal kindness; never be condescending but make real friends with the poor." As a couple or as a family, we must look beyond ourselves and extend our kindness and love to those around us who are in need.

These simple bits of advice from St. Paul are as timely today as they were when he first wrote them. People have not changed that much in essence in the last two thousand years.

St. Paul ends this part of his Epistle with these words: "Do all you can to live at peace with everyone." That's good advice at any time.

The Kingdom of God

When I was young, the phrase "the Kingdom of God" meant no more to me than "the Riviera" or "the Alps." These were just names that had nothing to do with my life. Later, I thought it referred to heaven or the afterlife. In recent years I have learned from the Church that the Kingdom of God begins in this life and continues on to the next. So what is the Kingdom of God?

Father Richard McBrien says that the Kingdom of God is God's redeeming presence. This is the best definition I have heard to date. God is actually doing something real to us, in this world, right now. The redeeming action of God is alive all over the place: in the café, at the supermarket, at school and at work.

Wherever there is real love, caring, self-sacrifice and sharing, we can be sure that God's redeeming love is present and is taking us farther than we could ever hope to go on our own.

Most of our modern civilization speaks to us in the language of cynicism and despair. This is not the

Kingdom of God. Those of us who are tired of the current cynicism and endless despair can help to create the Kingdom of God through our Christian attitudes and through our refusal to buy into the negative values of the day.

We may not realize it, but by virtue of our baptism, you and I are empowered by the Holy Spirit to bring the Kingdom of God to our world.

Father McBrien writes that "The Kingdom of God exists wherever God's will is at work. And God's will is at work wherever people are faithful to the command that we love one another as God first loved us." He goes on to say,

> The redemptive presence of God can be found in everyday personal experiences. Wherever people love one another, forgive one another, bear with one another's burdens, work to build up a just and peaceful community, wherever people are of humble heart, open to their creator and serving their neighbour – God's redemptive and liberating presence is being manifested. God's Kingdom and loving rule is in operation there.

We are all involved in promoting the Kingdom of God. Our work here on earth is not merely to endure this "vale of tears" while we are still alive. Our real work is to help by our daily actions and relationships to build up the Kingdom of God here and now. This is the Church's message. It is not a new message. It is a message that takes us back to the time of Jesus.

All of us can feed the hungry, visit the sick, comfort the sorrowful and welcome the stranger. These people are in our midst, waiting for the Kingdom of God to become manifest ... through us.

God and the Universe

I welcome all new information about the universe. This information comes from scientists and tells me more about God.

Old Testament people thought that the world was flat, surrounded by water, and that a giant dome in the sky kept the water from falling on the earth. This dome had gates or floodgates that opened when it rained.

You won't learn much science from the Bible, but then, you are not meant to. Somebody has written, "The Bible is not a book about how the heavens go ... it is a book about how to go to heaven."

Though God does not change over the ages, our concept of God certainly does.

The updated Hubble telescope can look billions of years back into time through space. One recent discovery sticks with me. Scientists have sighted the formation of a star that is ten times the size of our solar system. This fact is very difficult for us to imagine. How can we imagine God, who is infinite, when we cannot even imagine the size of the universe, which is finite?

We have always known, and the Church has always taught, that God reveals himself to us through nature and through the physical universe. Yet God goes far beyond that. God has revealed himself through his Son, Jesus. That happened a mere two thousand years ago. Knowing that the formation of the universe and of our planet took place several billion years ago, Jesus' time on earth is a recent event.

St. John writes, "No man has ever seen God." But Jesus himself said, "Whoever has seen me has seen the Father." Jesus is alive. He is risen from the dead. We can have a relationship with him here and now.

We encounter God through Jesus in countless ways. At Mass, Jesus shares himself with us through the Word and through the Eucharist. We also meet Jesus in the people who cross our path each day.

The universe may be vast, but God loves every one of us individually for all time.

The Cloud of Unknowing

Countless references to *The Cloud of Unknowing* led me to search out this unusual book. A spiritual classic, it is claimed by Christians of all traditions.

Nobody knows who wrote *The Cloud*, but it was probably an English country priest who penned the work around the year 1370. Today, over six hundred years later, the book is popular among those who profess an interest in meditation. Much of the inspiration for the current "centering prayer" school of spirituality is found in this book.

The book is an amazing combination of quaint medieval spirituality and timeless exciting spiritual insights that seem to be written especially for today's Christian. Certain thoughts jump out at the reader and demand to be meditated upon. There is nothing frantic or fanatical in the advice "Learn to love God with quiet eager joy, at rest in body as in soul." God is in the quiet depths of our being, at our "centre," yet covered by a "cloud of unknowing" that can be penetrated only by love. The overall message of the book is a hopeful one. My favourite quotation is this: "For it is not what you are or have been that God looks at with His merciful eyes, but what you would be."

The book was written as a guide for those who are seeking to better their spiritual lives. It is popular today because people want to move beyond the recitation of formulas in prayer. Many are exploring the meaning of prayer. What is prayer? When is one praying? Can ordinary people pray in ordinary situations? Can a book like *The Cloud* help us? Can we become contemplatives without becoming monks? Should we? Why? How can we tell the difference between God's inner promptings and our own imagination? Can we make a retreat without going anywhere? How do we make contact with God in the depths of our own being? These are some of the questions that *The Cloud of Unknowing* addresses.

For someone who grew up using set formula prayers, it is not easy to set out on new and uncertain paths. Yet finding new ways to pray is an intriguing way to build our relationship with God.

The problem is that God speaks ever so quietly. We must give up some things to listen to God – such as our own thoughts and even the peaceful feeling we might get from prayer. So says the author of *The Cloud*.

Many books on spirituality recommend that we find a guide to help us progress in the spiritual life. CDs and DVDs may be helpful, but a personal connection with a spiritual director would be ideal.

Today, Christians are experiencing a renewed interest in spirituality. *The Cloud of Unknowing* was written against the backdrop of the Black Death in Europe. Today we live with the threat of ecological ruin, natural disasters, war and epidemic illness. In times such as these, our quest for God takes on new urgency. Our attention turns to the hidden presence within us who is our love, our hope and our salvation.

Finding God in the City

In the past, many serious-minded people ran from urban centres and took refuge in deserts and mountains in a very personal quest for God. They elected to live out their lives in seclusion, perfectly content to let the rest of the world go by. This type of life is commendable for the occasional person who wishes to find God in silence and solitude.

Many classic books on spirituality emerged from a rural, monastic setting. But it is useless today to tell someone that if they mix too much with other people they risk losing their holiness or virtue. Such a pious thought simply is not true. What's more, for most of us it is impractical.

So what about the rest of us poor souls who must find God on city streets and in the midst of a confusing and rapidly changing world? Do we have less chance of finding God than the hermit does? I don't think so.

Our civilization is increasingly an urban one, but we do not yet have an adequate urban spirituality. We need someone to write a book called *The City*

Dwellers' Way to God to take up where books like *The Imitation of Christ* left off.

Even more than a book we need a new mentality that helps us sort out events in the world around us and see that God is very much a part of the modern city. God hasn't changed over the centuries, but we have. We are 21st-century men and women living in an electronic age. We are what Marshall McLuhan has called "postliterate." How do "postliterate" men and women find God today?

If modern people's way to God is to be through the electronic image rather than just through the printed page, the Christian churches need to offer more evangelization through television and the Internet. In this way they will help build a spirituality for modern people that fits their lives.

Meditation and Well-Being

Recently I was reading a magazine article about the dangers of high blood pressure. To counteract this dangerous and hidden threat to human life, the article said, "many doctors advocate relaxation techniques such as meditation."

For centuries the Church has been advocating meditation for the spiritual life. The message has been slow to get through. The first problem is that the practice is seen as the exclusive domain of the monk or the professed religious; the second is that it has been seen as something that is good for the soul but not necessarily for the body or for one's whole being.

Many recent influences have helped improve meditation's image: the growing interest in Eastern religions, a holistic concept of people that no longer emphasizes the body-spirit dichotomy, and the modern health and fitness movement which looks to meditation as a path to well-being.

In some ways, people both inside and outside the Church see meditation as something secular rather than as a religious practice.

But whether secular or religious, whether Christian or non-Christian, meditation is good for both soul and body. Detaching oneself from daily concerns and seeking interior peace is healthy and beneficial from both a psychological and a physical point of view. We need to seek out God in meditation, not because we are monks or because we have made a commitment to the religious life, but because it draws us into God's presence. Leaving behind our daily preoccupations, we place ourselves in silence before our God.

Norman Vincent Peale writes about the importance of filling our minds with positive thoughts so we are not overcome by the dark side of life. He says, "The person whose mind is stayed on God is kept in perfect peace because his mind rises above insignificant matters." When we spend a few minutes every day doing some form of meditation, we will find peace.

When my son was four, he asked me, "How come Holy God speaks so low that you can hardly hear him?" I replied that God does not talk to us in words but in thoughts and ideas in our minds and hearts. Meditation gives us the opportunity to listen for God in the silence.

Faith and Darkness

Christian faith is based on the existence of a God we cannot see; we live in the darkness of faith. In every age, people have asked, "Why does God hide himself from our senses?" Why do we see only "through a glass darkly," as St. Paul expressed in one of his letters to the Corinthians?

Countless writers and filmmakers have tackled the subject of faith. In his book *The Devil's Advocate*, novelist Morris West asks, "What is faith?" He answers that faith is "a blind leap into the hands of God. An inspired act of will which is our only answer to the terrible mystery of where we came from and where we are going."

In Ingmar Bergman's *The Seventh Seal*, a highly symbolic film set in the Middle Ages, a knight returning from the Holy Land passes through a country plagued with the Black Death. Meeting Death on his way, he asks, "I want God to stretch out His hand toward me, reveal Himself and speak to me. Is it so cruelly inconceivable to grasp God with the senses? Why should he hide Himself in a mist of half-spoken promises and unseen parables? I call out to Him in the dark but no one seems to be there."

The Knight also says to Mary, a character he meets on his travels, "Faith is a torment, did you know that? It is like loving someone who is out there in the darkness but never appears, no matter how loudly you call."

Leading theologians also explore this question. Jesuit theologian Karl Rahner asks, "Have we ever tried to love God when we seemed to be calling out into emptiness and our cry seemed to fall on deaf ears, when it looked as if we were taking a terrifying jump into the bottomless abyss, when everything seemed to become incomprehensible and apparently senseless?"

From these accounts and from our own experience we know that faith in God is one of the great mysteries of life. God exists not because we feel his presence (or don't feel it). God's relationship with us is in a realm beyond feelings. Some writers have said that God is probably closest to us when he seems most distant. Many saints found that earlier in their spiritual lives they received great consolation from God and felt his presence keenly. As their spiritual lives matured, God seemed to draw away from them. Some of them experienced great periods of dryness or what St. John of the Cross called "the dark night of the soul."

Making the decision to welcome Christ into our lives does not necessarily mean that we will feel God's constant presence every day. Faith in God is not blind faith, but an ongoing journey of ups and downs that leads us to God. As St. Augustine said, "Lord, I believe. Help my unbelief!"

No Free Lunch?

How is it that so many people have no problem accepting God's justice, yet they have a real problem accepting God's mercy? They feel that, because they are "bad" or have been "bad" in the past, sooner or later God is going to get them.

The problem is that we imagine we can think as God thinks. If we can never forgive someone who has done a terrible thing, then how can God forgive that person?

The parable of the workers in the vineyard makes no sense to us. A group of workers arrives in the morning to work in a vineyard. They go at it all day in the burning sun. More workers arrive throughout the day. One group strolls in late in the afternoon and puts in one hour of work. When all the workers line up to be paid, they all get the same amount of money. This is justice? Not by our standards. Thankfully, God's love is not measured by human standards.

Society tells us that there is "no free lunch." What we get, we work for. Nobody is going to hand things to us. Advertisements that start off with the words FREE, FREE, FREE are not really giving anything away to us, they are merely trying to get our attention.

Though we have grown up with it, many of us have missed the point of the Good News. Jesus has paid the price for all of us, both saint and sinner. The size of our sins and offences is nothing compared to the infinite love and mercy of God. Jesus said that he came for those who are sick, not for those who are well. All of us are unhealthy in some way, so we all need him.

Just when things seem hopeless and people seem to have lost sight of God, the Good News knocks us off our feet with the startling announcement that there *is* a free lunch – or, better, a free banquet – to which we are all invited. Jesus has purchased tickets for all of us. None of us is forced to attend. We are free to turn down the invitation.

Some people walk around as though they are already dead. The Good News has put no joy in their hearts and added no lightness to their steps. Then, one day, when they least expect it, something changes. In the words of C.S. Lewis, they are "surprised by joy." Everything falls into place. Jesus is everything they have been missing – the way to God and to the eternal banquet.

Peak Experiences

We are fascinated by the lives of the rich and the famous, perhaps because we consider our own lives to be rather humdrum. We live in safe, quiet places, yet we read spy thrillers about men and women who live dangerously in exotic locations. We seek excitement, adventure and escape from our daily round of family chores and business duties by sitting in front of the TV.

Much of life involves repetition. Many people are trapped in jobs that seldom allow their spirits to soar to new heights. As Thoreau put it, "The mass of men lead lives of quiet desperation."

Yet for all the repetition and ordinariness in our lives, all of us have moments when we rise above our daily routine, and experience rare moments of insight. These moments have been called different things by different writers. Abraham Maslow calls them "peak experiences." Rollo May calls them "moments of creation." Whatever we call them, they are spiritual.

Perhaps we have gone through a bad period of confusion, not knowing where to turn or where to go with our lives. We pray. Nothing happens. We continue to pray. Suddenly, one day we experience a tremendous sense of peace and tranquillity. Our whole life comes into sharp focus and we know with perfect clarity the direction we are going to take. We are lifted above ourselves, perhaps just for an instant. In that instant we know that our prayer has been answered and that the Spirit has given us the insight we needed to act wisely.

These moments of grace are not the exclusive property of famous people or saints. They come to everyone because "the Spirit moves where it wills." Curiously, these insights often come when we least expect them. After focusing on a problem for a number of days, we decide to rest and unwind. The answer to our dilemma may then come to us in sleep, or when we are thinking of other things.

During these moments of enlightenment we realize that the answers to our problems lie within ourselves. Ultimately, no one can solve our problems but ourselves. The Spirit moves from within our own depths to help free us from our infantile fears and fantasies. These "peak experiences" and "moments of creation" are evidence that God operates in our lives, often without our noticing it.

Loneliness and Hospitality

"Are you lonesome tonight?" sang Elvis Presley. Thousands upon thousands of people no doubt answered secretly in their hearts, "Yes, I am. I am very lonely." Yet chances are they did not share their feelings with anyone.

Like many emotions, loneliness is not easily detectable in others. People with a broken ankle from a skiing accident get all kinds of sympathy and attention as they sit near the fire in a ski lodge. Sitting next to them may be a woman who is broken-hearted because her husband has recently died. We do not see her pain so we do not enter into it. She cannot wear a sign that says, "Talk to me. I am devastated."

Yet in any gathering we can be sure that there are many people who are terribly lonely, suffering from some loss or facing the prospect of living alone for the first time in their lives.

Older people who live alone are often in great need of a simple phone call. The content of the phone call is immaterial. The call itself means that somebody remembers them and cares enough to make contact. The new low rates on long-distance phone calls are a blessing for people whose children have had to leave home in search of work. Those who go "away" often feel very much alone in a strange environment as well.

People cannot survive without friendship. We all want to belong to somebody or something. We have a need to share our story with another. So many people simply want somebody to listen to them. I become a real person to another only when I reveal myself. Those who know about my good points and my failures can joke with me because they have accepted me as a fellow human being. Many lonely people do not have this feeling of camaraderie with anyone.

Many of our parishes need to work on their hospitality and welcoming. Christians should be able to find a worshipping community where they are greeted, accepted and loved. We have a long way to go to see ourselves as a community of love and worship rather than a loose collection of individuals attempting to save their souls by fulfilling their Sunday obligation.

My neighbour is the one who needs me now. When we are sensitive to the people around us, we will likely find that our own loneliness vanishes when we attend to the loneliness of others.

Three Images

Our image is that total impression of ourselves that we knowingly or unknowingly project to others. These days, people are more image conscious than they were in previous ages of history.

I believe that there are three images that we contend with: our image of ourselves, the image that others have of us, and the image that God has of us.

Our image of ourselves dictates our behaviour. If we think that we are shy and inferior, we will act accordingly. Thankfully, our image of ourselves can change. This is what conversion is – turning away from one set of beliefs to a new way of looking at ourselves and our world.

The image that others have of us can be misleading. People can classify us as straitlaced or wild, as intellectual or foolish. The problem with such an image is that it is often superficial. Deeper qualities are overlooked. Some people may have an entirely false and misleading image of us because we have never taken the trouble to share anything of ourselves with them. Communication destroys false images and helps put the right ones in place.

God's image of us is the most significant one. God has known and loved us since before we were born, and holds each of us in the palm of his hand. We are precious in God's sight. The image helps us improve the image we have of ourselves.

Many people are held prisoner by the false image that they have of themselves. Others are held prisoner by the false image that people have of them. Freedom consists in casting out the old, false image of ourselves and taking on our true image. We can come to see our true and complete image only if we open our eyes to the image God has of us.

Living Above Confusion

Being a Catholic Christian can be very confusing these days. There are many groups in the Church and several ways of thinking. There are liberals and conservatives, traditionalists as well as those who want the Church completely overhauled.

The other day a friend reminded me of a basic reality. "The Church is divine," he said, "but the human side of it is all politics." This situation has not changed since the time of Jesus.

In the midst of all this clamour, people are still asking, "What must I do to be saved?" or, "What is most important in our religion?" Jesus was asked the same question. His answer was so simple that many people did not take it too seriously. He said, "Love God and love your neighbour as you love yourself." Jesus also placed a great deal of importance on the idea of hospitality: welcoming others into your life. He did not say, "Bring your family to church once a week and you will be saved."

Jesus' answer involved the community and our re-lationships with others. Being a Christian is by no means easy. If it were as simple as being physically in a church building for one hour a week, he would have made that clear to us.

The difficult part comes when the priest sends us out of the church into the world for another week. Some people think that you can turn off your "religious button" till next Sunday. Others gradually realize that our relationship with God and with others continues wherever the week's work takes us. Helping others is not easy. It can make constant demands on our time, our talents and sometimes our money. It never ends. As Jesus reminded us, "the poor you have always with you."

As long as we are trying to love God and to love our neighbour, we know that we are on the right track, no matter what century it is or who the current Pope may be.

A new pope may have a different point of view on a number of things, but this does not change our mandate from Jesus to love and care for others. We should never become obsessed with church policies or politics to the extent that we lose sight of Jesus. Jesus is the reason for everything. There is an expression now used at Christmastime that says that Jesus is "the reason for the season." He is also the beginning and the end of every thing on earth. Our personal relationship with Jesus is the most important thing in our lives.

Further changes in the Church may come soon or they may not come for generations. The Church is not a "win-lose" situation for liberals or conservatives. Jesus wants us all to be saved. For this he gave his life.

Uncertainty

Despite all our technological advances, life remains uncertain. Insurance companies were created to protect us and our families because we have no idea of what may happen to us or our possessions in the future.

The stock market is uncertain, and is affected by world events which themselves are uncertain. Natural tragedies happen at random times. Terrorists and their actions heighten fear and make us even more aware of our vulnerability.

Life has always been this way. We simply don't know. Every night on TV, "experts" make predictions about the future, but they don't really know anything for sure.

Christians choose to rely totally on the love and mercy of God. There is no other answer to the question of where we are going after this life is over for us.

God sent his Son to give us hope and to show us the way to the Kingdom: love God and help our neighbour. Some of us live in this world only for a short while; others live a long life. How we live is more important than how long we live.

Despite all the uncertainty of this life, the Christian can live with joy. Jesus brings Good News: salvation is here and it is free.

This Good News of Jesus is what keeps us going in a very uncertain world. If the cross is a symbol of suffering, it is also our main symbol of hope. The first thing that a person receives just before baptism is a sign of the cross on their forehead.

Scripture says, "The people who walk in darkness have seen a great light." This is the light of Jesus and it is the only thing that matters.

God's Forgiveness

Recently, I came across a book called *Prayer* by a favourite writer of mine, Dom Hubert van Zeller, from Downside Abbey in England. He wrote more than 50 books of devotion, biography, scripture and fiction. He is also a sculptor and a cartoonist – a very talented man. He has been called a one-man renaissance.

The thing I like about van Zeller is that he can be profound without using big words or cumbersome phrases. Anyone can read van Zeller and understand him. He is an excellent communicator and knows his audience very well.

In *Prayer*, he is trying to help ordinary folks like you and me to pray better.

He takes the Our Father phrase by phrase and helps us to understand its inner meaning. When he talks about God forgiving our trespasses, he says that we have a concept of God that is overly influenced by the human emotions we see in people around us. I am slow to ask God's forgiveness because I think of God as a stern parent, "who is likely to get angry, who has to be kept in a good mood, whose children have to walk on tiptoe and sit up straight." "Do I think of Him," asks van Zeller, "as touchy, given to misunderstandings, liable to hold it against me that I have failed so often in the past?"

The important thing to note, says van Zeller, is that "whatever other fathers are like, this Father loves me all the time and can never change … and He always goes on loving me even when I have sinned against Him and am hanging back from repentance." This is based on two absolute facts: first, that God is love, and second, that God cannot change. Van Zeller continues,

> It would be a complete mistake for me to imagine that I have somehow got to calm down the just wrath of a grieved parent, or that I have to wait a while for His anger to cool off and for His sadness at my failure to lessen with the passing of time. God loves me when I have not sinned, but He loves me also when I have sinned. He would not be God if He stopped loving me.

It is difficult for us to understand God because we have only human experiences and human relationships to go by. We make assumptions about God that are simply not true. God is love; he cannot unlove. The moment of reconciliation with God is always now. God holds no grudges. He carries no resentment. He is not limited by the pettiness of humankind. Like the father of the prodigal son, he is always waiting for us on the road with open arms. Before we take the first step back to him, God has already forgiven us.

Being Healed and Holy

Many people today are looking for techniques for relaxation and healthy ways to deal with tension, stress, anxiety and depression. The mind, the body and the spirit are so interconnected that in order to be "whole" or holy we have to learn to pull ourselves together. Interestingly, the words *heal*, *whole* and *holy* all come from the same root word in English. Becoming healthy is the first step on the road to wholeness and holiness.

We can learn a lot about relaxation from the Eastern religions. Yoga and breathing exercises help to slow the movements of the body and bring us to a sense of peace. To "centre" oneself is to seek peace at the centre of one's being. Many people achieve this centring process by silently reciting a mantra – a word or phrase that helps us to stay focused. A common mantra is the Jesus Prayer: "Lord Jesus Christ, Son of God, have mercy on me, a sinner." Mantras can be used effectively in times of stress, grief, loss, fear, tension and pain (physical, psychological or spiritual). Saying a mantra such as "The Lord is my shepherd" or "Come, Lord Jesus" when we are feeling stressed can keep us calm and in control.

Our lives are busy. We live in the midst of confusion and noise. Learning how to rise above the confusion allows us to be whole. Being whole, we are both healed and holy.